Slower:
50 Ways to Thrive in a Fast World

Carl Honoré in the Media

"The global guru on the Slow Movement."
Globe and Mail

"An in-demand spokesman on slowness."
The Wall Street Journal

"The unofficial godfather of a growing cultural shift toward slowing down."
Huffington Post

"The godfather of the Slow Movement."
ABC News

"Inarguably, the world's leading evangelist for what has become known as the Slow Movement."
CBC Radio (The Sunday Edition)

"An international spokesman for the concept of leisure."
Newsweek

"A verbal magician, conjuring concepts with no new idea too complex to capture."
Australian Financial Review

Cover design and ebook design by Simon Williams.

Book design by Matthew Bin.

ISBN: 978-1-8382574-1-5

For information about special discounts or bulk purchases for sales promotions, premiums, educational use, or fund-raising, please visit

www.carlhonore.com/contact

Table of Contents

Introduction

> *"Anything worth doing is worth doing slowly."*
> ***Mae West***

People often tell me

> *"I love the idea of slowing down. I want less rushing, distraction and busyness in my life. But I just don't know how to do it. Where do I even start?"*

This book answers that question. It contains the tools you need to slow down and thrive in a fast world.

Embracing slowness can make you happier and healthier, more connected, dynamic and creative. It can unleash a better you—at home, at work and everywhere in between.

I know this from personal experience. I used to be a roadrunner, racing through life instead of living it. But then I slowed down, and everything fell into place.

Since then, I have dedicated my life to helping others reconnect with their 'inner tortoise'. I travel the world to write books, make TV and radio programs and deliver talks and workshops on the power of slowness.

But don't worry, I'm not a slow fanatic. On the contrary, I love speed! Faster is often better—we all know that.

But not always. Sometimes slowing down is the best option.

SLOW is a mindset.

It means doing everything at the *right* speed: quickly, slowly or whatever pace works best. It means being present, living each moment fully, putting quality before quantity in everything you do.

This book will help you cultivate your own version of SLOW.

I have distilled everything I know about slowing down into 50 simple tips. Feel free to work through them in whatever order feels right for you. But I do recommend setting aside one week to test drive each tip. Give it the full seven days. Beside every tip you will find a blank page. You can use this to write about what it felt like to put the tip into practice. Then, at the end of the week, ask yourself: Did this tip help me slow down in a good way?

If yes, keep on doing it. If no, drop it and move on.

Remember, the aim is *not* to end up performing all 50 tips all the time. That wouldn't be very slow! Pick the ones that work for you and then tailor them to fit your life.

Consider also teaming up with other people. Slowing down is easier and more fun when you do it with someone else. Try the tips with a friend, partner, colleague or family member. You could even create your own online community.

Whether you use this book alone or with other people, you will notice the benefits right away. You'll feel less harried and more serene, less distracted and more focussed, less tired and more energised. In other words, you'll be on your way to mastering the art of SLOW. Your days of running around like a headless chicken will soon be a distant memory.

The truth is that it *is* possible to slow down in a fast world. And not only is it possible, it is the best thing you will ever do for yourself and the people around you.

Trust me, you can find SLOW. One step at a time...

1. Check

At random moments, stop what you're doing and consider how fast you're doing it.

You might be taking a shower, reading a document at work or eating lunch. Whatever it is, pause, create a real moment of awareness and ask yourself:

Am I doing this too fast? Would I do it better and enjoy it more if I slowed down?

If the answer is no, and you're operating at the right speed, then just carry on as before.

But if the answer is yes—as it often is!—take three deep, calming breaths. And then go back to the task at hand more slowly.

This week, deploy the speed check at least twice a day.

2. Notifications

These days, we go everywhere with a weapon of mass distraction in our pocket—or hand. Smartphones fill every moment with stimulation: games, videos, social media, notifications, news updates, endless messaging.

This constant barrage of interruptions takes a toll on our health, happiness and ability to focus.

A simple way to dial down the distraction is to turn off notifications on your devices. Every missive and message will still reach your phone. The difference is you'll be looking at them when it suits you. Not when it suits other people.

Result: you'll find it easier to give the things that really matter the time and attention they deserve.

This week, turn off all notifications on your phone for a few hours each day.

3. Nature

Eco-therapy. Green time. Wilderness cure. Forest bathing. Whatever you call it, being in nature is a tried-and-tested way to slow down.

Spending time in green spaces makes you feel calmer, happier and less stressed. It can also improve memory, creativity and concentration.

This week, spend at least 20 minutes per day in the great outdoors. Wander through a forest or fields, meadows or moors, hills or mountains. Hang out in a park. Or just potter in your garden.

4. Awaken

Many of us are so exhausted that the mere idea of waking up earlier feels like a kick in the teeth. Trust me, it's the exact opposite.

Rising earlier can make your morning routine more relaxed. It gives you more time to linger in the shower, choose the right clothes, savour breakfast, get the kids ready for school.

Waking earlier is an easy way to carve out the time you need to slow down and start the day feeling calm, energised and in control.

This week, win the morning by rising 15 minutes earlier than normal.

5. Cook

In the modern world of microwaves, ready meals and home delivery, cooking is a lost art. Yet there is so much to be gained from making your own food. Cooking from scratch, touching the raw materials, feeling your way through a recipe, tasting, adjusting, engaging all the senses, can be a soothing release.

You can make a very simple meal—roasting a tomato, sprinkling it with a little sea salt and arranging it artfully on a plate. Or pull down one of those recipe books gathering dust on the shelf and whip up a multi-course feast.

Either way, make cooking a moment of real joy. Put on your favourite music or podcast. Or turn it into a communal affair by enlisting others to help with the chopping, grating, stirring, simmering, tasting and seasoning. Don't cook to impress—just enjoy the act of cooking itself.

This week, make one meal from scratch every day.

6. Phone

Picture a conversation between two people: friends, lovers, colleagues, siblings, a child and parent. Studies show that if a phone is visible during the encounter, those two people keep the conversation on a more superficial level.

The phone doesn't have to ring or vibrate or light up. Just being within view is enough to weaken the human connection.

That means it pays to keep phones out of sight when chatting to someone in person. Hide them in a pocket or a bag or under a magazine. That small act will make a big difference to the tone, tenor and texture of your exchange.

This week, hide your phones every time you have a face-to-face encounter with another person.

7. Puzzle

One of my favourite ways to slow down is doing jigsaw puzzles.

I can sit there for ages, hunting down elusive pieces, mapping out which sections to tackle and in what order. I forget the clock, my mind wandering here and there.

Puzzling also brings people together. Everyone wants to lend a hand so you end up sitting alongside members of your household and even visitors, joining up pieces, chatting away or in companionable silence. I've had some wonderful conversations with my children while puzzling.

This week, spread out the pieces of a giant puzzle on a table somewhere in your home and watch it turn into an oasis of Zen.

8. Letter

When was the last time you wrote a letter by hand? Typing is so much quicker that we almost never put pen to paper anymore.

Yet writing by hand is a richer, more resonant way to communicate. Its slowness inspires reflection. On life. On your feelings. On what you want to say and how and why you want to say it.

The time and attention you put into a handwritten letter also sends a powerful message. It tells the recipient: You matter to me. Writing by hand is a sign of respect, even an act of love.

Waiting for a handwritten letter to arrive through the mail can also bring its own pleasure. You have something to look forward to. You escape the tyranny of instant gratification.

This week, send two handwritten letters to people who really matter to you.

9. Values

When life gets too fast, you lose touch with who you are and what you stand for. You cruise along on autopilot, following someone else's script.

One solution: slow down, think deeply and reconnect with your own values.

Studies show that even just writing about your values can make you calmer, more focussed and more successful in life.

Here's how to do it: Sit in a quiet, comfortable place and write down five values that matter to you right now. Your list might include Loyalty or Faith or Family or whatever. Write as much as you like about one of them. The next day, write about another value. And so on.

On days six and seven, ask yourself this question: Are there changes I can start making right now to live more in line with my values? Write down those changes and try to act on them.

This week, set aside 15 minutes each day to write about your values.

10. Breathe

One way to slow down your life is to slow down your breath. Deep breathing is a balm for mind and body. It curbs anxiety and stress, fosters calm and sharpens concentration. It takes only a few minutes and can be done almost anywhere.

Here's how:

Sit or lie down in a quiet, comfortable spot. Close your eyes. Put one hand on your tummy and the other on your chest. Take a normal breath, in and out. Then breathe in deeply and slowly through the nose. Notice your tummy swelling under your hand. Hold the breath for a second or two. Then breathe out slowly through your mouth, noticing how your tummy subsides. Repeat several times until you find a soothing rhythm.

This week, set aside five minutes three times a day to perform a slow breathing exercise.

NB: Learning to breathe slowly can be the gateway to another very way good way to slow down: meditation.

11. Gadgets

Technology has colonised the home, with everyone on their own screen, pinging messages from room to room.

One way to roll this back is to stash away your devices in a Gadget Box. You can make one by tarting up an old basket from the shed. Or a discarded shoebox. Whatever you choose, place your Gadget Box near the front door—but not so near that a burglar can reach it through the letterbox!

Everyone entering the home must drop their devices into the Box and leave them there during certain times agreed in advance.

This week, set aside a few hours each day when all your devices are salted away in a Gadget Box.

12. In-Between

When your schedule is tightly packed, you end up leaping from one thing to another. No time to reflect on what you've just done or plan for what's coming next.

Building in time between activities allows you to slow down, catch your breath and reset. Even a few minutes can make a big difference.

This week, add five minutes of downtime between the major items on your To-Do list.

13. Notes

Look around any meeting or lecture and almost everyone is taking notes on a laptop or tablet. Typing is faster than writing by hand, so using a keyboard makes perfect sense, right?

Wrong!

Taking notes by hand is actually more efficient—thanks to its slowness.

You can type fast enough to take notes verbatim. But no-one writes that quickly with a pen. When you take notes by hand, you have to process and précis what you're hearing in the moment. And that helps you understand the material better. It also means you remember it better later on.

This week, take handwritten notes during every meeting or lecture you attend.

14. Less

Having it all is a recipe for hurrying it all. A crammed schedule forces you to race through life instead of living it.

One solution: do less by creating a Not To Do list.

Start by scanning your calendar to find things you can drop. A non-essential meeting. A party you can duck out of. An underwhelming Netflix show you could skip. Place it on your Not To Do list and move on.

Keep copies of your Not To Do lists. Glancing at them later is a useful reminder that a lot of stuff that seems undroppable at the time can actually be dropped without the world coming to an end.

This week, move one item a day from your To Do list to your Not To Do list.

15. Monotask

Multitasking is a myth. The human brain cannot think meaningfully about more than on thing at the same time. Not even the female brain!

When you 'multitask', you're really just toggling back and forth between tasks. Result: you make more mistakes and take much longer than if you did one thing at a time.

Cultivate the art of monotasking. Find a time when you can work free of interruptions. List all the tasks you want to achieve—and then work through the list, one task at a time.

If something urgent comes up, put aside the task in hand and focus on the urgent work. If you reach what feels like a natural stop point, even if that means leaving a task unfinished, move to the next thing on the list. Remember, the key is training your full attention on one thing at a time.

This week, spend four hours per day monotasking.

16. Serve

"If you want to go fast, go alone. If you want to go far, go together."

This old proverb is a reminder that helping others goes hand in hand with slowing down.

A fast life is a selfish life. When you get stuck in roadrunner mode, the only thing that matters is getting through your day.

When you slow down, you begin to *see* other people. You are able and eager to connect and be of service. Studies show that helping others also boosts your health and happiness. In other words, the world is a better place—for everyone!—when we all slow down and look out for each other.

This week, spend a few hours volunteering in your community. Serve in a soup kitchen, collect litter in your neighbourhood, visit residents in a care home or inmates in a prison, tutor a child from a disadvantaged background, do a shift at a community garden.

Slow down, give back and find your better angels.

17. Listen

Listening is a dying art. Often when it's our turn to listen, our mind wanders—Is that my phone? Am I running late? When will this person stop talking so I can say what I want to say?

Listening is one thing you cannot accelerate. No matter how much of a rush you're in, you can never listen faster. Humans are not podcasts: we don't come with a button that makes us speak more quickly.

To listen—and I mean *really* listen—you have to slow down to the tempo of the person speaking to you. You have to be present.

Next time you're in a one-on-one conversation, make a real effort to listen carefully. Ask questions (everyone loves to feel interesting!). Using your own words, weave back into the conversation the highlights of what the other person has said to you. Notice how much more you get from the encounter.

This week, take a slow approach to listening in at least one conversation every day.

18. Eat

Many of us eat too fast. We guzzle and gobble. We inhale food while doing other stuff: gazing at a screen, driving, walking down the street. Fast eating is joyless and can lead to weight gain and eating disorders.

By contrast, eating slowly and mindfully brings more pleasure and makes you happier and healthier.

Cut a favourite food into bite-sized chunks. You might choose mango, chocolate or cheese. Notice the colour and texture of the chunks. Now smell the food, inhaling deeply. Is your mouth watering, your mood brightening? What memories do the aromas evoke? Now place the first chunk on your tongue. Notice its weight, its texture, the way the anticipation is building exquisitely. When you can't take it anymore, start chewing, slowly, deliberately, noticing how the flavours evolve in your mouth. Bask in the sensory pleasure of the moment.

This week, do this exercise with two different foods. And try to bring the same slow intensity to the rest of your eating—without freaking out your fellow diners!

19. Stroll

Flânerie is a wonderful French word. It means strolling with no goal beyond exploring, observing and savouring. It's the opposite of power walking.

When you channel your inner *flâneur* or *flâneuse*, you notice flowers and trees, clouds in the sky and hills on the horizon, how the light dances on water or across the windows of a building. You hear birdsong and the laughter of strangers. You take pleasure in what others are wearing and doing.

Big thinkers, from Woolf to Nabokov, have always hailed the creative power of an unhurried walk. As Nietzsche said: "All truly great thoughts are conceived while walking." Thich Nhat Hanh, a Zen master, believed that mindful strolling brings spiritual clarity and heals both the walker and the world.

This week, go on three long, leisurely walks with your phone turned off.

20. Nap

The Japanese call it *inemuri*. In Spanish it's a siesta. Whatever word you use, napping is on the rise in the modern workplace.

And I'm not talking about a bottle of wine followed by a two-hour snooze! That kind of fun is best kept for your slow vacation.

I mean a leaner, meaner, more modern siesta. Maybe a glass of water followed by 10 to 20 minutes of sleep—as recommended by NASA—to return to your desk refreshed, rebooted and raring to go.

This week, take a short nap after lunch every day.

21. Email

Emailing in haste often causes confusion, or offence, leading to more and more emails. Far better to slow down and get your message right the first time round.

When Abraham Lincoln wrote an angry letter, he would leave it in a drawer. When his temper had cooled, he would re-read the missive and decide whether or not to send it.

Why not adapt Lincoln's technique to email?

The next time you finish writing an important message, don't push Send right away. Instead, move it to your Draft box. Take a short break. Do some breathing exercises. Or go for a walk.

Then, reread the email to be sure it says exactly what needs to be said in exactly the right way.

This week, channel Lincoln whenever you write an important email.

22. Make

Making things by hand, whether a clay pot or a loaf of bread, slows you down. Knitters often compare their hobby to yoga. Studies show that the rhythmic, repetitive dance of the needles lulls you into a calm, almost meditative state.

Making can take many forms: carpentry, sewing, ceramics, cooking, painting, building a bicycle, weaving, metalwork, bookbinding. Whatever lights you up.

This week, make something by hand. You might begin a new project, or finish off one that's been lying abandoned in a closet. Either way, set aside 15 minutes per day for making.

23. Meet

High-level meetings at Amazon often start with a period of silence that can last up to 30 minutes. Which is a lot less weird and wasteful than it sounds.

During that silence, Amazon executives read through detailed reports and prepare their arguments. So when it's time to start speaking, everyone knows what they want to say and how they want to say it.

Result: meetings that are short and efficient.

This week, take a leaf out of Amazon's book. Agree with your colleagues to start three meetings with a period of silence, banning screens and phones wherever possible. Use the time to calm down, focus and marshal your thoughts.

24. Play

In its purest form, play is a profound way to engage with the world. To stretch your mind, body and soul. To find other people and yourself. When you do something with a playful spirit, for the sheer joy of it, you forget the clock and remember who you are.

Play is SLOW in action.

This week, set aside 15 minutes per day for play. Pick an activity that clears your mind and leaves you feeling recharged and fulfilled. It could be arts and crafts, sports, building a train set, baking, yoga, fixing stuff, gardening. Avoid screen-based play and recreational shopping. Forget the clock and just be playful.

25. Quote

When trying to slow down in a fast world it helps to have a little inspiration on tap. One way is to collect pro-slow quotes from famous people. Here are some old favourites:

There is more to life than increasing its speed. (Gandhi)

Anything worth doing is worth doing slowly. (Mae West)

The hurrier I go, the behinder I get. (Lewis Carroll)

Haste denies all acts their dignity. (Dante)

Slow down, you move too fast, you got to make the moment last. (Simon and Garfunkel)

Two of the most powerful warriors are patience and time. (Tolstoy)

This week, write down your favourite pro-slow quotes. Drop them into conversations. Slip them into emails. Whisper them to yourself when you need a little pick-me-up.

26. Audit

In this fast, busy world it's easy to slip into autopilot, skimming through life without ever asking whether you're living the right life for you. That's why it pays to carry out a personal audit from time to time.

Here's how: Block off some time outside work. Settle into a quiet, comfortable place. Reflect on the following questions for as little or as long as feels right to you:

Am I living the right life for me or just going through the motions? Where do I want to be in 5, 10, even 20 years? How can I stop stressing about myself and start being of service to others?

Be ready for your mind to wander off towards your grocery list or the latest celebrity gossip. Don't beat yourself up. Just notice the detour and gently steer your thoughts back to those big questions.

This week, do one personal audit.

27. No

Saying yes to everything locks you into a life of hurry and haste. You get so busy that you end up running to stand still.

Saying no stops you being a doormat and frees you up to focus on the stuff that really matters. Warren Buffett, the fabled investor, once said: "The difference between successful people and very successful people is that very successful people say no to almost everything."

Cultivate the art of saying no. Start by practising on strangers, in low-stakes scenarios. Say no to a chugger in the street, to the barista urging you to try a new topping, to the cold-caller hawking insurance on the phone. Then graduate to friends, family and colleagues.

Get comfortable saying no. And remember that "No" or "No, thank you" can be a full sentence. You don't always have to justify yourself. The more you explain, the more you start to waffle and doubt your own stance. So keep your no short and sweet.

This week, say a firm but polite no twice a day. Try to do this with a different person each time.

28. Sleep

Sleep is the ultimate way to slow down—what could be slower than spending time in the land of Nod? It's also a magic bullet for wellbeing.

Getting enough sleep sharpens concentration, improves mental and physical health and boosts productivity. It can also help you maintain a healthy weight.

This week, make sleep a top priority every night.

Stop looking at screens at least one hour before going to bed. Avoid late-night snacking or drinking. Keep all electronic devices outside your bedroom. Fill the time before turning out the lights with activities—soaking in the bath, making love, reading a good novel, chatting to your nearest and dearest—that leave you feeling relaxed and serene.

29. Spontaneity

Packed schedules are not only exhausting, they also make it hard to be spontaneous. Because every moment of the day is already mapped out.

Yet the richest experiences are often unplanned and unscripted. Keeping a light schedule frees you up to savour accidental pleasures, stumble on a big thought or a small detail, indulge a whim.

This week, block off one afternoon when you plan nothing in advance. When the time rolls round, do whatever fits your mood. Or just enjoy doing nothing at all.

30. Think

When you feel calm and relaxed, your brain shifts into a richer, more creative mode of thought that psychologists call Slow Thinking. The smartest people in history have always understood the power of slowing down, taking time and letting the mind wander. Charles Darwin described himself as a "slow thinker". As did math whiz Maryam Mirzakhani. Albert Einstein was famous for spending ages staring into space in his office at Princeton.

This week, set aside 30 minutes every day to retreat somewhere quiet and slip into Slow Thinking mode. Set yourself a question or two and then let your mind go where it goes.

31. Music

When did you last listen to an album from start to finish in one sitting? I know, right.

These days, we hop from track to track, artist to artist, shuffling, skipping, pressing Next before the last song has even finished. This turns listening to music into a nervy hunt for optimisation.

One remedy: listen closely to an album from beginning to end.

Instead of striving to curate the perfect playlist, you embrace and explore the path forged by the artist. You discover tracks that take time to fall in love with. You relax and your mood lifts.

This week, pick two albums in whatever genre floats your boat: rock or rap, soul or ska, country or classical, jazz or jungle. On separate days, sit down and do nothing more than listen to one of the albums uninterrupted from start to finish.

32. Learn

Learning a new skill fills you with zest and purpose. It also takes time. You have to slow down, focus, ask questions, listen, take risks, practice, make mistakes, reflect.

This week, set aside 30 minutes per day to master a new skill. Study an unfamiliar language. Cook a new dish. Learn a craft. Try a new sport. Savour being an eager pupil again.

33. Rhythm

Life is good when you slow down to honour your own rhythms. Is there anything more delightful than slipping into the right groove?

This can be hard to do at work so pick one of your days off this week and make it My Rhythm Day. Forget the clock and just go with the flow.

Eat when hungry. Rest when tired. Do whatever you feel like doing: working out, playing cards, baking, watching a movie, hanging out with someone.

Whatever you do, do it at your own pace and in your own time.

34. Journal

Milan Kundera once said that "when things happen too fast, nobody can be certain about anything, about anything at all, not even about himself."

Journaling is one antidote to that problem. Recording your thoughts in a diary can curb stress, boost mood, sharpen concentration and forge lasting memories.

It also helps you reconnect with yourself. Slowing down to look inward and listen to the whispers from your heart helps you figure out who you are and how you want to be in the world.

This week, set aside 20 minutes every evening to write a journal. Reflect on life. Marinade in deep thoughts. Ponder your next step.

35. Frugal

Fast living is expensive. You spend money to save time, to heal your body and mind, to distract yourself from the emptiness of life on autopilot.

That's why slowing down often goes hand in hand with spending less. When you live at your own pace, you always have enough time. Your body and mind are in rude health. You don't need retail therapy because you love your life.

Being frugal doesn't mean being a cheapskate or a killjoy. It means resisting the shopping impulse and spending money more wisely. It also means understanding that the best things in life are usually free.

This week, hold two zero-spending days. Fill your time with activities that cost nothing yet make your heart sing.

36. Share

Oscar Wilde once quipped that "after a good dinner one can forgive anybody, even one's own relations." That's because sharing a meal binds human beings together. It's no coincidence that the word '*companion*' comes from the Latin for "with bread".

When life gets too fast, we end up eating alone. In the car, in bed, *al desko*, on the sofa watching TV. A good way to slow down is to break bread with others.

This week, share a meal with someone else at least once per day. At work, at home, wherever. Turn off all phones, sit at the table together and let the conversation flow.

37. Sketch

When did you last take the time to stop and stare? These days we're in such a rush that we seldom look at things. I mean *really* look at them. We scan, glance, skim or scroll—and then move swiftly on.

Sketching forces you to look, look harder, then look again. You notice contours, colours, textures, the play of light. You explore your own responses to the person, object or landscape that you're drawing.

Sketching, in other words, slows you down. It clears and quiets the mind and sharpens focus.

The best part is you don't have to be Picasso to sketch. My own doodling never gets a public airing! What your final sketch looks like really doesn't matter. What matters is the act of sketching itself.

This week, set aside 15 minutes a day to sketch an object, person or scene.

38. Stack

Looking for a fun ritual to put your phone in its place? Try 'stacking'.

When you go out for a coffee or a meal with friends, stack up your phones on the table. Cover the pile with a garment. The first person to cave and start using their phone pays the bill for everybody else.

It's a simple way of saying: We have this moment here together now. We will never have this moment again. Let's not spoil it by trying to be in several other moments at the same time. Let's stop fiddling with our phones and be fully together.

This week, give stacking a try during three social gatherings.

39. Declutter

The world is awash with stuff that drains our time, money, attention and energy. That's why decluttering goes hand in hand with slowing down.

After all, less is more.

Let's be honest: most stuff is unimportant. Over the years, it just builds up in your life, like limescale in a kettle. And you learn to live with it.

Truth bomb: You don't have to live with it!

You can chip away the limescale and flush it down the sink. From clutter in your home to activities that no longer light you up, having a good clear-out can be both cathartic and soothing.

This week, get rid of one piece of 'clutter' every day.

40. Gratitude

Practicing gratitude saves you from the vortex of FOMO. You stop envying the curated lives on social media and start appreciating the good things you already have.

Being grateful has been shown to boost mood, self-esteem and life satisfaction. Strengthen relationships. Bolster physical and mental health. Improve sleep.

In short, practicing gratitude slows you down in all the right ways.

Every morning or evening, write down a few things you're grateful for. These can be as simple as 'I had a coffee with my dad' or 'I met a nice person at the gym'. Or you can express gratitude to others, such as thanking your partner for preparing a lovely meal or a colleague for bailing you out at work.

This week, find three things to be grateful for each day.

41. Silence

Silence is rare in the modern world. Noise and distraction hound us everywhere we go.

Yet silence is golden in so many ways. It sharpens concentration, boosts learning, gooses productivity and deepens self-awareness. It builds calm, clarity and patience. Silence and slowness are close allies.

This week, set aside 15 minutes every day to sit in silence somewhere.

No screens, no music, no podcasts. Just you and your thoughts. Let your mind wander. Grapple with big questions. Ponder the small stuff. Notice how the silence helps you reset and reboot.

42. Moments

Many of us have forgotten how to enjoy the moment. We rush through everything. We multitask, trying to be in several moments at the same time. We dash through life instead of living it.

When you slow down, even the tiniest moment can be a feast for the senses and a balm for the soul. Looking at a beautiful sunset. Biting into a perfect peach. Cycling with the wind in your hair. Exchanging smiles with a stranger in the street. Smelling freshly-mown grass. Sharing a joke with a neighbour. Sipping a divine cup of coffee. Hugging your partner or child.

This week, put those small moments centre stage. Make a real effort to slow down, be present and open yourself up to what's happening right here, right now.

43. Books

Most of us spend a lot of time reading these days—but usually in fast mode. We skim, scroll, scan, skip, taking little joy from the act itself. It's reading as a tool, a means to an end.

Sinking into a good book, fiction or non-fiction, is a very different kind of reading. The sound and fury of the outside world melt away as you enter a silent dance with the author. Reading books slows you down. It can also improve your sleep, memory and empathy.

Napoleon once declared: "Show me a family of readers, and I will show you the people who move the world."

This week, set aside 30 minutes each day to curl up with a good book (or a trashy one!). Leave your phone in another room. Read at your own pace—it's not a race and there's no deadline. Give the words, the story, the ideas your full attention.

Reflections

44. Market

According to a recent survey, 90 percent of British children aged 6 to 12 do not know that strawberries come from plants. Talk about losing touch with the land!

Farmers' markets are a lovely place to reconnect with the slower rhythms of nature. You learn so much about food—where it comes from, how it grows, what's in season, what goes well with what—by talking to the people that produce it.

The food in farmers' markets is also natural and unprocessed, which means it tastes better and is kinder to your body and the planet.

This week, shop in a farmers' market. Try all the samples—that's what they're there for! Chat with the vendors. Buy ingredients that make your spirits soar and then come home and cook up a slow meal.

45. Compassion

Time pressure makes us quicker to anger and more focussed on our own needs. To be less compassionate, in other words.

Compassion is the ultimate win-win. It helps the recipient. But it's also good for the person being compassionate. It curbs stress and boosts health and happiness. It can even give a sense of meaning and purpose—the first step to changing your own life for the better.

Compassion comes in many forms. Chatting to a homeless person on the street. Inviting a lonely neighbour round for tea. Lending an ear to a bereaved friend.

This week, commit a random act of compassion once a day.

46. Art

Art is the highest form of human expression. It invites us to pause, observe, dream, feel, reflect. It cultivates a spirit of play and curiosity. Art can slow us down and help us be better.

The best way to look at art is slowly. Inspect it up close, from afar, from every angle. Contemplate and savour the fine details. Ask yourself: Is this artwork telling a story? What feelings or memories does it arouse in me?

This week, pay one visit to a museum or gallery. Choose three works and spend at least five minutes looking at each. And I mean *really* looking. If you can't go in person, call up three pieces of art on a large web browser at home. Block out all distractions, slow down and focus on what's in front of you. Let the art work its slow magic on you.

47. Relationships

We are social animals. Bonding makes us happy and healthy. It also gives life meaning, texture and joy.

Relationships cannot be accelerated. You can't make someone fall in love with you faster because you want to get married next month. You can't forge a close friendship today because you need a travel companion tomorrow. You can't make a child explain her anxiety in the three minutes before you leave for work. There is no website where you can download trust or team spirt.

Relationships thrive on two things that only slowing down can deliver: time and attention.

This week, find two hours you would normally fritter away on social media, TV or recreational shopping. Spend that time instead face-to-face with another person. A friend you haven't seen for a while. A relative going through a hard time. A colleague you'd like to get to know better.

Put away your phones and go for a long walk or sit on a park bench or have a meal together.

48. Games

Video games are fun. But they're all about staring at a screen, often in a room by yourself.

Traditional games deliver the fun without the screen. They bring us together in the real world. They also curb stress and boost cognition. In other words, they slow us down in all the right ways.

By 'traditional' game, I mean a screen-free contest of reflexes and wits, such as cards, chess, board games, dominoes or charades.

This week, set aside two evenings or afternoons to play old-school games with your partner, family or friends.

49. Garden

Nature never rushes. Trees, plants and flowers grow at their own pace.

That makes gardening a good way to slow down. Sinking your hands into the soil, sowing and tending your own crop, watching it grow and blossom, is both soothing and gratifying. Gardening curbs anxiety and stress, boosts mood and improves attention span. It also teaches patience.

There are many ways to garden. If you have the space, you can plant your own flower bed or herbs or vegetable patch. If not, you can grow plants in pots on a windowsill or pitch in at a local community garden.

This week, spend two hours gardening. Roll up your sleeves, engage all five senses, tap into the deep, rolling slowness of nature.

50. Observe

Hergé, the creator of *Tintin*, once said "the street is a museum for everyone." In other words, slowing down to watch the world go by is one of life's great pleasures.

People watching is endlessly entertaining. It tickles our curiosity: What does that man with the umbrella do for a living? Are these two people siblings, friends or colleagues? What is that couple arguing about? People watching reminds us that we are not alone, that we are part of a something bigger, that humans never stop being fascinating, infuriating and inspiring.

Every day this week, set aside 15 minutes to sit in a public place and do nothing else but watch the world go by.

Conclusion

"In a world addicted to speed, slowness is a superpower."

Carl Honoré

Congratulations, you made it! By now, you're well on your way to mastering the art of SLOW.

But this is not the end of your journey. In our roadrunner world, the pressure and temptation to speed up are relentless. And no one is immune. From time to time, you will fall off the wagon and rush needlessly. And that's okay. Never lose heart. Just dust yourself down, take a deep breath or two and then push the Reset button.

That's where the 50 tips come in. Every single one can help you slow down when you're moving too fast. But don't just use them in emergencies. Identify your favourite tips and make them a permanent part of your routine. (Personally, I use the speed check all the time and am a big fan of cooking and saying no.)

Remember, too, that you are not alone. Everyone yearns to slow down in this fast, frenetic world. And there is strength in numbers. So team up with others and slow down together.

Before we part ways, I want to leave you with two final thoughts.

First, SLOW is good. It may seem redundant to say so at the end of a book like this, but it needs saying. Over and over. Why? Because the taboo against slowness still runs deep in our culture.

Second, please keep in touch. Write to me via my website or on social media. Tell me (and the world!) how you're getting on with the tips.

Together we can defeat the virus of hurry. We can all become better people leading better lives in a better world.

We just have to give SLOW a chance.

Let's do it!

Biography

Carl Honoré is an award-winning writer, broadcaster and voice of the Slow Movement. His books have been published in 36 languages and landed on bestseller lists around the world. His two main-stage TED Talks have racked up millions of views. While researching his global bestseller, *In Praise of Slow*, Carl was slapped with a speeding ticket.

Other Books by Carl Honoré

Carl's books help you build a happier, healthier, more productive life:

In Praise of Slow: Challenging The Cult Of Speed *(rest of world)*
In Praise of Slowness: Challenging The Cult Of Speed *(USA)*

The foundation text and handbook of the Slow Movement. Dissects our compulsion to hurry and chronicles a global trend toward putting on the brakes.

The Slow Fix: Solve Problems, Work Smarter And Live Better In A World Addicted To Speed

A powerful recipe for tackling complex problems in every walk of life, from health and relationships to business and politics. Learn how to avoid short-term quick fixes in favour of lasting solutions.

Under Pressure: Putting The Child Back In Childhood

A guide to helping children thrive in an impatient, perfectionist world. Aimed at parents, teachers and anyone else keen to give kids a childhood worthy of the name.

It's The Journey Not The Destination (rest of world)
Slow Adventures (USA)

An illustrated book for parents and children to discover the wonders of the world through Slow travel. Features four slower modes of transport: bicycle, train, boat and your own two feet.

30 Days To Slow

A practical, step-by-step workbook to help you build a calmer, richer life. Another great companion to In Praise of Slow.

The Power of Slow (CD)

A how-to course packed with tips, techniques and exercises for slowing down in a fast world. Spoken by Carl.

Bolder: Making The Most Of Our Longer Lives

A book about ageing—how to do it better and feel better about doing it. A spirited takedown of ageism and the cult of youth.

To learn more about Carl's books, digital courses and more, visit www.carlhonore.info.

Bring Carl To Your Organisation

If you've enjoyed this book, why not have Carl work with your organisation?

He travels the world to address audiences ranging from CEOs, entrepreneurs and sales professionals to teachers, academics and doctors. His keynotes are dynamic, inspiring, informative and full of humour. He also delivers workshops and does consulting work.

To book Carl, send an email to carl@carlhonore.com.

www.ingramcontent.com/pod-product-compliance
Lightning Source LLC
Chambersburg PA
CBHW070048040426
42331CB00034B/2633

* 9 7 8 1 8 3 8 2 5 7 4 1 5 *